C000121394

LONDON TAXI DRIVER SLANG

Compiled by GRAHAM GATES

BSON
OOKS
ONDON

5 Sidney Square London E1 2EY
Tel 020 7790 4737
Fax 020 7790 7346
email absonbooks@aol.com
web www.absonbooks.co.uk

ABSON BOOKS LONDON
First published June 2011
© Graham Gates
Designed by Bill Vickers

Printed by Gutenberg Press, Malta
ISBN 9780902 920910

INTRODUCTION

should come as no surprise that the London's taxi trade is rich in slang; there have been cabs and cabmen its streets for nearly four hundred years.

The selection of terms has been confined to those in current or recent use, many of which have been around generations. Some are not exclusive to taxi drivers, others may be recognisable only to discover they hold different meaning within the trade.

Hackney Carriage, Cab or Taxi ?

These three terms feature within this work, the last two being interchangeable. This simply reflects the way drivers talk about their job. In order to avoid confusion there follows a definition of each: -

Hackney Carriage: - the oldest term, in use since the seventeenth century. Possibly from Saxon, via Flemish and ultimately the French "hacquenée", meaning "an ambling horse". The word "hack" is still used today to describe an old horse and laws relating to the London's taxi trade still refer to the "Hackney Carriage Acts".

Cab: - also from the French, "cabriolet", a light, two-seater carriage drawn by a single horse.

Taxi:- an abbreviation of "taximeter cab". Although the taximeter was invented in 1891 it wasn't until 1907 that a law was passed requiring its installation in all cabs. By that time the internal combustion engine was well on the way to replacing the horse and the use of the term "taxi" became widespread. If the vehicle you're travelling in hasn't got a meter, it's not a taxi.

A

Admirals	Dolphin Square; mansion blocks bearing the names of admirals
all-in	total daily takings before deductions for diesel, cab rent etc.
All-London driver	one possessing the coveted **Green Badge**
All Nations	the cab shelter in Kensington Road, near where the Hall of Nations once stood during the Great Exhibition of 1851
American Workhouse	Park Lane Hotel, Piccadilly; once popular with our American cousins
appearance	a periodical appointment when undertaking the **Knowledge**
A-Z Mansions	Queens Club Gardens; mansion blocks set alphabetically
Aztec Temple	Vauxhall Cross Headquarters of MI6, due to its architecture

banker	a regularly requested fare
aze	Bayswater Road
ell and Horns	cab shelter in Thurloe Place SW7, after a former nearby coaching inn
e lucky!	one cab driver's farewell to another
ilker	'low-life' who legs it without paying, see **runner**
ill	cab driver's licence; also brief or kite
inder	long wait on a rank for a fare
lown out	when the queue *for* cabs is shorter than the queue *of* cabs
Blue Book	the bible of **knowledge boys** since 1911.
lue trees!	shouted warning of speed-cops hiding behind trees.
owler hat	City gent
Box of Tricks	Euston Station
rass	prostitute; from rhyming slang, *brass nail*
Bridge, the	taxi rank at London Bridge Station

broom	pass on an unwanted job to the next cab on the rank
Bull Ring	the roundabout with the Imax cinema, Waterloo
bullseye	fifty, especially a £50 note
bung	tip or a bribe
burst	chucking out time at popular venues
butterboy	novice cab driver; sometimes just "a butter"
buzzbox	noisy taxi

C

cabology	cab drivers' gossip, opinions, philosophy even!
cage	passenger compartment
call over	answer an examiner's questions during a **Knowledge** appearance
canary	a driver who works a suburban rank, aka **yellow badge**
Canary Land	London's outer suburbs
cargo	another term for **punters**

Carriage Office	The Public Carriage Office (PCO) until recently the body responsible for regulating London's taxi trade (see page 33)
casher	driver, usually a **butterboy**, who boasts about the money he's taking
caso	brothel; from the Italian "casa", a house
catch a cold	earn little money during a shift
changeover	time and place where a **double team** swap their shared cab
Chapel, the	cab shelter in Wellington Place behind the church, see **Nursery End**
Chelsea Gasworks	Chelsea House, Lowndes Street, because it's round
Cherry Blossom Roundabout	Hogarth Roundabout on the A4 where that brand of shoe polish was manufactured
choke off	close the partition behind the driver to end an argument
chop up	nip in front of another driver and nick his fare
Circus, the	specifically Piccadilly Circus
Clipboard Johnnies	operators around nightspots for minicab companies illegally touting for business
clock	most commonly used slang for the taximeter, others include cuckoo and ticker; see **hickory** and **zieger**

cockle	ten, usually £10 - or a tenner
Colditz	unkind name for the former **Carriage Office**
Cole Porter	a driver who works long hours ("Night and Day" by Cole Porter)
come out	start a shift, as *"wot time joo come aht terday?"*
come out of a drain	a surprise fare; one which appears from nowhere
comics	road maps, like your faithful A-Z
confessional	pull-down passenger seat behind the driver
Connaught	stranger, unknown driver from rhyming slang, *"Connaught Rangers"*
cotton-up	length of cotton and two pins to find the shortest route between two points on a street map; used as an aid in some Knowledge Schools
cream fare	profitable job; a long journey or a generous punter
Cri, the	rank near the Criterion theatre
cricket seats	pull-down seats mounted on the partition
Cross, the	rank at Kings Cross or Brent Cross
cruise	look for work on the streets; an older term is 'mooch'

dead ride	retuning empty from a long journey
Dead Zoo	Natural History Museum
Den of Thieves	London Stock Exchange, aka "*Thieves' Kitchen*"
Diesel Alley	see **Green Badge Valley**
diff.	differential gear which gives the London taxi its tight turning circle
Dilly, the	Piccadilly and the surrounding area
dirty dozen	twelve back streets linking Regent Street to Charing Cross Road
dive	insalubrious cafe, pub or club
divide	partition separating driver and passenger
dogfight	daily battle with London's traffic
do a man over	steal another driver's rightful fare
do a rank over	take a fare close to a rank where drivers are waiting with empty cabs
do the green	only way a **canary** can become an **All-London driver**
double team	day man and a night man who jointly own a taxi

drive	stringent driving test London taxi drivers must first pass
drive-in	protest when drivers take to the streets in their cabs
drop	monetary tip
drop heavy	punter who tips well
droschky	Russian-Jewish origin for cab
duck and dive	running a job through back streets to avoid traffic

E

early-day man	driver who starts his shift in the small hours
Eastern, the	Liverpool Street Station, aka the Liver
extras	surcharges shown on the meter

F

ace	driver who frequents the same rank, shelter or caff
'are	passenger or a hiring
Feeder	secondary rank used to "feed" a main rank
Feeder Park	500 cab-holding rank at Heathrow
Fifty sixes	days intervals between appearances when starting the **Knowledge**, these reduce to twenty eight, twenty one & fourteen days
flag	'for hire' sign, aka the stalk
flag fall	initial charge shown on the taximeter
flash lot	smart, new taxi
Flat-Iron Square	small triangle of land at the junction of Union Street & Southwark Bridge Road
Flower Pot	Covent Garden area of former flower market
flyer, a	job to airport, usually Heathrow
Flyers, the	Heathrow Airport

fouling the rank	joining a rank at an incorrect point
four-hander	four punters at one hiring
frarney, a	rain or a rainstorm; from rhyming slang "France & Spain"
Fritz, the	Ritz hotel, Piccadilly or its rank in Arlington Street
full-flat	method of renting where the driver keeps the cab all week
full-house	answering all an examiner's questions correctly on a "Knowledge appearance"

G

gaff	any entertainment venue likely to provide much cab work
Gaff Street	Shaftesbury Avenue, location of many theatres
Gantville Cowboys	see **Green Badge Valley**
Gas Works, the	The Houses of Parliament; hot air at extortionate prices
Gateway to the South	Balham, SW12, from a comedy song of 1959 by Peter Sellers
Gaza, the	The Ideal Cafe in Ebury Bridge Road SW1, run by friendly Arabs
General Roy's	canteen at the old **feeder park** at Heathrow

George, the	rank outside the pub at Hampstead Green
get off	come away from a rank with a fare
get one in	get a job from Heathrow into Central London
get one out	get a job outside the Greater London area
get out	receive your taxi licence and badge
Gherkin, the	Swiss Re building in St Mary Axe, aka 'The Erotic Gherkin'
ghost	driver who haunts the same rank (noun or verb)
Glass Egg/ Glass Helmet	City Hall, home of the Greater London Authority; aka "The Mayor's Testicle" and "Wobbly Jelly"
Goldberg's Green	pun on "Golders Green"; like our trade it has a large Jewish presence
grapes of wrath	haemorrhoids; the bottom line is they come with the job
greasegun	cheap café
grease up	stop for food
green badge	worn by drivers entitled to work **all London**. Also a term for the driver himself
Green Badge Valley	Gants Hill, Newbury Park, Clayhall, etc, reputedly heavily populated by London taxi drivers; aka **Diesel Alley**

H

hair dryer	hand-held speed gun
half-flat	method of renting a cab for part of a day
handful	£5 or alternatively five punters in the cab at once
hanging up	waiting for a fare other than in an appointed place
Hangover Square	Hanover Square , once the location of various night spots
Harabs	Harrods; a pun on its former Egyptian owner
hickory	taxi meter; from rhyming slang *"hickory, dickory, dock"*
high game	cheating fellow drivers
hole-in-the-wall	side entrance to Victoria Station, Wilton Road
Honda	Japanese tourist
honeypot	The West End
hoorays	posh, young blokes out on the town
Hospital Square	Queen Square, one-time location of four hospitals
hurry-up job	when the punter is pressed for time

im'n'er	man and a woman, at one hiring
In and Out, the	Naval and Military Club, St James's Square
in-and-out job	a round trip
Inside-Out Building	Lloyds Building, Leadenhall Street
instalment mixture	rain, supposedly bringing more work to the **musher** paying off his cab
interview	question **punters** on their destination to find a job to the driver's liking
Iron Lung	the urinal in Regency Place (best hold yer breath!)

ob	a hiring or a passenger
John Bull	a pull; being arrested or pulled over by the law
ourneyman	one who drives a rented cab

K

kipper season   January and February when the trade is flat see **mini kipper**
knocker   driver who owes money, generally to a cab garage
Knowledge, the   'The Knowledge of London', the exams that all cab drivers must pass
knowledge boy   one going through the above exam system

L

last knockings   tail end of a queue requiring cabs
late man   one who starts his shift around 6pm
leatherarse   driver who works long hours, aka 'copperarse'
legal, a   flat fare, no tip
linkman   hotel doorman, from the days of carrying a link or lantern
livery, in   when a cab's bodywork is decked out in a single advert
loaded rank   one with cabs waiting for fares

local, a	short journey after a long wait on a rank
long cut	route chosen for speed rather than distance
long-day pills	said to be taken by a **leatherarse** to keep him going
long 'un	lengthy shift worked by a driver used to more regular hours
Loo, the	Waterloo Station; often reached by having to pass water
love job	when expected to take family or friends for free
lying foul	queuing beyond the designated area of a rank

M

macaroni	'pony', i.e. £25
magic carpets	pedestrian crossings
Magic Circle	area round Piccadilly Circus
Magic Roundabout	Shepherds Bush Green, which is triangular
mark	taxi rank, from its road marking;
mate	term of address to any cab driver who's a **Connaught**

mince pie	the London Eye; from rhyming slang
mini kipper	the August downturn in trade see **kipper season**
minorcas	walkers; those who choose to walk rather than take cabs
Museum, the	rank at the British Museum
mush/musher	owner-driver; rhymes with "rush" not "push"
mushers' lotion	rain; see **installment mixture**
mystery	any young woman travelling alone

N

nick	any police station
night man	driver who works when the highest tariff operates
No-Hope Gate	Stanhope Gate, where the rank to the Dorchester has been shortened
Northern, the	King Cross Station and rank
Northerns	collective term for the above plus St Pancras and Euston Station
Nursery End	shelter near Lords Cricket Ground; see **Chapel**

O

Oak, the	once-favoured cabbies' watering-hole near Royal Oak Station
old dears	intrepid, genteel old ladies who often travel with back-breaking luggage
old dog	older taxi still working the streets
on mileage	cab rental where the driver pays a charge for every mile driven
on point	cab at the head of the rank; another term is 'point cab'
on the clock	cab rental where the driver keeps a percentage of the meter takings
over the hump	a job to or from the City via the Angel and City Road
over the water	"sarf" of the river (*never* "south") which we will go to if asked nicely

P

Paddy Fields	affectionate term for Irish areas like 'County Kilburn'
Pancake, the	St Pancras Station
Pandemonium	London Palladium

Penguin Island	rank at junction of Camden High Street & Camden Road
peters	luggage; from rhyming slang "*Peter Pan*", can or a tin trunk
PG Tips	Palace Gardens Terrace; from the brand of tea with the same initials
pick-out job	when a punter chooses a cab from the middle of a rank
pie-and-mash job	radio-cab slang for a cash fare, not one on account
Pier, the	cab shelter adjacent to Albert Bridge
Pigshit Farm	offices of company responsible for much of the external adverts on cabs
Pill Island	Harley Street/Wimpole Street block; full of private medical practitioners
pipe, the	London Underground system
plate	annual licence details affixed to the rear of every taxi
plot	modern term for a taxi rank
plot up	join a taxi rank; see **put on** and **rank up**
points	places which figure in questions posed to candidates on the **Knowledge**
Portuguese Tony's	Astral cafe, Regency Place, popular with cab drivers
punter	passenger; in common with bookies and prostitutes, cab drivers never have a customer

put on	join a rank; see **rank up** and **plot up**
put on the long rank	driving the streets looking for work

R

Raft, the	high-level rank at Victoria Station for Gatwick Express passengers
Rails, the	London's main line stations
rank up	join a rank; see **plot up, put on**
Rat Hole	rank at Waterloo Station
Rat's Hole	rank at Embankment Station
rattler	cab badly in need of overhaul
req.	'requisition'; to collect your badge and **bill** having completed the **Knowledge**
rest ranks	those few where exhausted cabbies can legally stop to recuperate
roader	long cab journey; see **schlep** and **dead ride**
roasting	waiting a long time on a rank, especially in hot weather; aka 'stewing'
ruck	quarrel; hopefully not a fight

run away	leave a slow-moving rank rather than wait for a fare
run it	in cab drivers speak, *"ow joo runnit?"* means, *"what route did you take?"*
runner	another term for a **bilker**
runners	**punters** without luggage who rush for cabs at railway stations
runs	routes to be learned when doing the **knowledge**

S

Saveloy, the	Savoy Hotel
scabs	minicab drivers who illegally tout for business
schlep	same as a **roader** but with more angst
score	twenty, usually a £20 note
set	road accident
set-down	point at which the **punter** alights
Shakespeare	a pub often requested as a **set-down** close to Victoria Station
Shark's Parade	Bedford Row, location of many top solicitors' offices

sherbet, a	a cab, from rhyming slang, 'sherbet dab'
shitcart	any cab in a poor condition
shock absorbers	several punters in the cab at once
show out	to hail a cab
stoomer	called to a job only to find the cab is not required
single pin	driving with a solitary **punter** on board
sixty-foot accordions	bendy-buses
sleepers	drivers who sleep overnight in their cabs or punters who fall asleep
smash	small change
snatched	cab reclaimed for non-payment of installments
snide	counterfeit money, cheques, licence-plates
splosh	cafe tea, warm and wet, like an English summer
spreadover	a shift which is part day and part night
stalk a job	or "*do a stalker*", drive a punter without engaging the meter
starving mush	owner-driver still paying for his cab
stepney	spare wheel; from the street in South Wales where first manufactured

stewed plums	anatomical affliction suffered by male cab drivers when **roasting**
stop note	list of faults to be put right before a cab can work again
strawberry	*"in a right strawberry"* means stuck in heavy traffic; a pun on 'jam'
sucking the mop	left on a rank when all other cabs have got off with a **punter**
suicide trikes	pedicabs; dangerous and expensive (they charge per person)

T

take the drop	accept a bribe
Temple, the	cab shelter in Temple Place
toe-biter	long wait on a rank in cold weather
touts	private hire drivers who illegally ply for hire.
trap	get a fare, as *"I trapped a job to the **Vic**"*
Trevors, the	Trevor Place, Square and Street
Tripe Shop,	Broadcasting House; this is more jocular than insulting
Turpentine,	the Serpentine, Hyde Park, sometimes just *"the Turps"*

U

unders	mechanical parts of a cab which need steam-cleaning at overhaul
under the horse's tail	top end of Queens Gate by the equestrian statue
uproar, the	Royal Opera House, Covent Garden

V

verbals	verbal abuse from punters & other road users
vic, the	Victoria Station and rank
volvo City	Stamford Hill, area where this make of car is popular

W

walkers & lookers	tourists not requiring cabs
walk-up job	where a punter approaches a cab whilst the driver is setting down another fare
Wall of Death	rotunda at the junction of London Wall and Aldersgate Street
wangling	learning to handle a cab prior to taking the **drive**, see **yardwork**
Washers & Polishers	Worshipful Company of Hackney Carriage Drivers. A gentle dig at this illustrious body who ceremoniously parade in incredibly shiny vehicles
wasp, the	acronym for **W**alpole, **A**nderson, **S**loane and **P**elham, a northbound route to South Kensington.
wedding cake	Queen Victoria Memorial outside Buckingham Palace, aka the "QVM"
Western, the	Paddington Station and its rank
wet doughnut	Princess Diana Memorial Fountain in Hyde Park
Wharf, the	Canary Wharf and its ranks
Wobbly Bridge	pedestrian Millennium Bridge
wrong 'un	job going in the opposite direction to one which the driver would prefer
wunner	£100

ard, the

former Public Carriage Office at Scotland Yard. *"Goin' up the Yard"* is still used to mean an appointment at Head Office

ardwork

part of the **drive** involving awkward manoeuvres in tight spaces

ellow badge

see **canary**

eiger

another term for the taximeter; from the Yiddish 'zeigen', meaning *"to show"*

A Butterboy's Guide to Cab Etiquette

Now that you are blessed with the coveted green badge and will henceforth be known as "*one who thinks he owns the bloody road*", it is time to let you in to the secrets of your chosen profession - the unwritten rules or 'ten commandments', which novice taxi drivers would do well to follow. I mean cab etiquette - yes, there is such a thing! Without it there would be anarchy on our streets. Let's leave that to minicabs and bendy-buses and behave instead in a manner befitting our proud traditions of nearly 400 years.

The Gospel According to St Fiacre

(Patron saint of cab drivers)

be thou always aware that an empty cab giveth way to a full cab

if thou art empty and without punter and another driver, also empty, permitteth thee to enter a street in front of him, thou shalt not take the next job on that street but leavest it for that driver

similarly, if thou art setting down and by so doing thou dost block the path of an empty cab behind thee, taketh not the next job but rather leaveth it to the man whom thou hast hindered

yea even though it be kipper season and thou art a long time jobless, thou shalt not overtake other empty cabs in front of thee, though their numbers be legion

if thou be with punter and thou knowest the whereabouts of other punters seeking cabs, thou shalt inform drivers of empty cabs in the vicinity of those punters so that these drivers may become similarly blessed

thou shalt not set down on a moving rank nor join a rank other than at the proper place, neither shalt thou unload alongside the point cab lest thou preventest him from getting off (vii)   *thou shalt not park thy cab on a working rank, even though thou art bursting for a pee and thy prostate be enlarged, nor to buy a present for thy girlfriend or wife or both*

(viii)   *thou shalt at all times keep the rank moving and not leave a chasm between thy cab and the next by ogling false idols on page three of thy newspaper, nor shalt thou stand talking to thy mate whom thou hast not seen since yesterday, lest it causeth the last man in line to lie foul*

(ix)   *thou shalt not broom an unwanted fare unto the driver behind thee but rather thou shouldst smile sweetly at the punter and take the job, yea even though it be south of the river*

(x)   *thou shalt not pick up a street fare within an hundred cubits (fifty yards) of a loaded rank but shouldst instead direct the punter towards the rank and the drivers thereon shall bless thee warmly*

A SHORT HISTORY OF THE LONDON TAXI

00's (early): Hackney carriages, or "Hackney Hell-Carts", appear on London's streets.

36: The first recognised cab rank established by Captain Bailey at the Maypole in the Strand (where St Mary-le-Strand church is today).

54: Oliver Cromwell orders the Court of Aldermen of the City of London to grant licences to two-hundred hackney coachmen.

57: These are revoked, some say for drunkenness, others that the aldermen favoured Cavaliers to Roundheads.

50: Restoration of the Monarchy leads to restoration of licences.

52: The Hackney Coach Office is set up to regulate the trade.

79: Introduction of "Conditions of Fitness" for hackney carriages.

68: The number of hackney licences increases to one thousand.

33 Duties of the Hackney Coach Office transferred to the Stamp Office.

34: Joseph Hansom patents his two-wheel cabriolet (the Hansom cab).

36: A four-wheel version follows - the "Clarence", aka the "Growler".

43: Control of the cab trade passes from the Stamp Office to the Commissioner of Police & the Public Carriage Office is formed soon after.

1851:	Introduction of the "Knowledge" by Police Commissioner, Sir Richard Mayne.
1875:	London's first cab shelter is built, thanks to Captain Armstrong.
1885:	The Public Carriage Office moves to premises in Scotland Yard.
1891:	Wilhelm Bruhn invents the taximeter.
1897:	Walter Bersey launches a fleet of battery-operated cabs.
1903:	The first internal-combustion engine cabs are introduced by Prunel, a Frenchman.
1907:	Regulations were introduced requiring all cabs to be fitted with a taximeter.
1911:	Publication of the first "Blue Book".
1913:	The great cab drivers' strike when cab fleet owners increased fuel charges by 60%.
1927:	The Public Carriage Office moves to 109 Lambeth Road and the first taxi school opens, run by the British Legion.
1946:	The last licence for a horse-drawn cab is issued (and rescinded the following year).
1966:	The Public Carriage Office moves to 15 Penton Street.
1982:	The Author gets his green badge.
2000:	Administration of the Public Carriage Office passes from the Metropolitan Police to Transport for London.
2010:	The Public Carriage Office is re-named "London Taxi and Private Hire Licensing" and re-locates to 197 Blackfriars Road, SE1.

The Public Carriage Office (1843-2010) R.I.P.

The PCO is no more. Once administered by the Metropolitan Police it fell into the hands of Transport for London (TfL), since when its gravitas has declined. From 2010 it became the more prosaic 'Taxi and Private Hire Licensing' relocating to the Palestra Building, in Blackfriars Road. Drivers have already begun the quest to find a suitable nickname. Suggestions include 'The Glasshouse', 'The Big Top', 'The (Glass) Shoebox' and 'The Plaster' because it's above a street called The Cut!

About the Author

'Sarf London boy,' Graham Gates, decided on a career change in 1979 in his thirties after seeing on the tell "The Knowledge" by Jack Rosenthal. Thus began two years of sleeping, dreaming, eating, drinking and living every street, traffic system, hotel, railway station, police station, court, prison, embassy, government office hospital, club, theatre, tourist attraction, sports venue, apartment block, store, restaurant and so on... within six-mile radius of Charing Cross. After a two-year struggle he finally got his coveted green badge. Now, aft 30 years as a London Taxi driver, he feels he is at last getting the hang of it.

Bibliography

Herbert Hodge - "It's Draughty Up Front" and "Cab, Sir?" (Michael Joseph,1938 & 1939)
Maurice Levinson - "Taxi" (Martin Secker & Warburg, 1963) Robert Buckland - "Share My Taxi" (Michael Joseph, 1968) G.N. Georgano - "A History of the London Taxicab" (Drake Publishers 1973) Philip Warren - "A History of the London Cab Trade" (Taxi Trade Promotions, 1995) and "The History of the Knowledge of London" (London Publishing Company, 2003) Alf Townsend - "Cabbie" (Sutton Publishing, 2003) and "The Black Cab Story" (The History Press, 2009)

Acknowledgements

I readily acknowledge I could not have done all this alone. My heartfelt thanks to Stuart Pessok, Managing Editor of "Taxi" Newspaper, for running a series entitled "We Speak Your Language" in 2006 in which he called for examples of cab slang in a noble attempt to keep the language alive. Thanks also to my fellow cabdrivers, some of whom I only know by nickname and who wittingly or unwittingly contributed to my collection which I began whilst on the Knowledge. Special thanks to Graham McGlashen who urged me to put pen to paper, or rather fingers to keyboard. Finally to my wonderful wife, Anne, the present Mrs Gates, for the use of her precious lap-top.

OTHER TITLES AVAILABLE

Language Glossaries
American English/English American
Australian English/English Australian
Cumbrian English
Gay slang
Geordie English
Hip Hop English
Home Counties English
Irish English/English Irish
Lancashire English
Military Slang
Playground Slang & Teenspeak
Police Slang
Prison Slang
Rhyming Cockney Slang
Rude Rhyming Slang
Scottish English/English Scottish
Scouse English
West Country English
Yiddish English/English Yiddish
Yorkshire English

History
The Death of Kings – A history of how the Kings
& Queens of England died

Who's Buried Where?
Discover where Royalty, the famous & the infamous
are buried

Literary Quiz & Puzzle Books
Bronte Sisters   Charles Dickens
Gilbert & Sullivan   Jane Austen
Shakespeare   Sherlock Holmes
Thomas Hardy

Available from booksellers or by contacting the publisher:

Abson Books London 5 Sidney Square London E1 2EY
Tel 020 7790 4737 Fax 020 7790 7346
email absonbooks@aol.com   web www.absonbooks.co.uk